TOO HURT TO CRY

Aileen Cunningham

Copyright 2021 by Aileen Cunningham
www.empowered2speakout.com

Printed in the United States of America 2021

ISBN 978-0-9993791-1-0

Publisher Speak Out Ministry

Cover design by **Jessica Land** thegfxco@yahoo.com

Book reviewed by **Jason Anderson** 1979jtanderson@gmail.com

All rights reserved. No part of this publication may be reproduced, stored in a retrieval system, included photocopying or transmitted in any form or by any means electronic, digital, recording, or another quotation.

New Testament Scripture copyright 1958,1987 quotations taken from The Amplified New Testament. Used by permission.

Old Testament Scripture copyright 1965, 1987 quotations taken from Zondervan Corporation. Used by permission.

The New King James Version of the Bible, copyright 1979, 1980, 1982 used by permission.

Scripture quotations marked KJV the King James Version of the Bible.

DEDICATION

This book is dedicated to my beautiful daughter Harmoni M. Cunningham. You are the greatest gift that God has given me. I'm forever grateful and honored to be your mother. Please remember that whatever happens in life, God has you covered and only has great things planned for you. You're the star of my heart and nothing is impossible concerning your dreams. Never stop believing in your dreams. My prayer is that God will continue to develop you into the young women that you are destined to be. Always remember my favorite scripture that will give you hope and encouragement during the rough times, Psalms 30:5 "For his anger lasts only a moment, but his favor lasts a lifetime! Weeping may last through the night, but joy comes with the morning.

TABLE OF CONTENTS

Introduction 1

Daily Reflection 1 - Believe Again 6

Daily Reflection 2 - Trust the Process 9

Daily Reflection 3 - Focus on Your Talents 13

Daily Reflection 4 - Fight Through the Storm 17

Daily Reflection 5 - See Beyond That Mountain 21

Daily Reflection 6 - Give Thanks 22

Daily Reflection 7 - Push Pass the Chaos 25

Daily Reflection 8 - Take Care of You 26

Daily Reflection 9 - Free Your Spirit 30

Daily Reflection 10 - Rebuild Your Faith 34

Daily Reflection 11 - Try Again 38

Daily Reflection 12 - Remove Any Doubt 41

Daily Reflection 13 - Prepare Your Mind for Your Harvest 44

Daily Reflection 14 - Forgive Those Who've Hurt You 48

Daily Reflection 15 - It's All Working Together for Your Good 51

Daily Reflection 16 - Choose to Trust 55

Daily Reflection 17 - Don't Accept the Valley 59

Daily Reflection 18 - Rise to the Top 64

Daily Reflection 19 - Believe 68

Daily Reflection 20 - Take Charge 72

Daily Reflection 21 - Move Forward by Faith 75

Summary - Say It Loud. Speak Life Over Your Mind and Body 79

INTRODUCTION

What do you do when you feel like the world is caving in around you? What do you do when you feel overwhelmed from bills, sickness, stress, loneliness, and the trials of life. You've tried everything to encourage yourself to keep going, but it's seems hopeless. What do you do when your tears have dried up because you've cried so many times over the years? What do you do when you feel like you're on a 24-hour emotional roller coaster ride with no way off? I wish I could provide you with one easy solution, but the truth is no manual exists for how we should respond to life's challenges. What I can share are the practical tools I used to overcome every struggle and setback in my life. My number-one weapon against adversity has been my faith and hope in knowing that God is in control. Knowing that my heavenly Father has complete control has given me the comfort and strength to move forward in life.

When I first started writing this book, I was in one of the darkest places of my life. I had relocated to Kansas City, Missouri, to live with my family after a divorce, being laid off from work, losing my home, having my car repossessed, and almost losing my mind. As you can imagine, my world was crumbling around me and I couldn't control it. To say I was afraid would be an understatement. I was terrified of what was happening. The worst part was that I had my six-year-old daughter, who didn't understand what was going on, with me and I tried to make her feel safe in the process. It's one thing to lose everything when you're living on your own, but it's another thing when your children have to suffer with you.

Back then, I didn't understand the paths of suffering that were happening in my life. At time, life seems so unfair. I must conclude that each experience was designed to make me stronger. They gave me the strength to be a better mother. After all, my job as a single mother is to protect and provide for my daughter. The fact that I couldn't do it caused me to hurt beyond what words could ever describe. No parent should ever have to worry about how they're going to feed and provide for their children, and put a roof over their heads. I often asked myself, "Wasn't it enough that I lost my childhood after surviving a dysfunctional background? Wasn't it enough that I was abandoned and rejected by everyone who said they loved me? Wasn't it enough that I barely survived after a failed marriage to a man who didn't value or respect me?"

Those experiences caused me to doubt everything I thought I knew about being a believer and having faith in God. I couldn't understand why God would allow them to happen to me and my innocent child. Over the years, I worked very hard to rebuild my life after experiencing abuse, neglect, and abonnement as a child, and recovering from a toxic marriage. I was at the bottom again and I couldn't cry another tear; I had had enough. For me, this was a dangerous place in which to be emotionally. The more I tried to cry, the more I felt numb in my body.

Due to the trauma I had endured, I realized that I had become numb from the inside out with no desire to push forward. That's a dangerous place in which to be. I understand that feeling because when you lose everything you've worked for, you can feel like a failure, defeated, and hopeless. This couldn't be farther from the truth. I now know that losing everything better prepared me to receive everything. It made me humble, more grateful, and aware of other people's sufferings. My hardships prepared me for my life's purpose. I now know that I survived every test for you. Our hardships prepare us to give hope and courage to others.

I created this book just for you. God wants you to know that your healing starts today. He wants to empower, encourage, and give you hope in your present situation. Life is more than struggling just to pay bills and surviving to exist. Life is about living out your purpose and taking hardships as life lessons. It's a mystery to us all who live in the now, but I'm determined to live in my best years now.

My prayer for you is that you allow every heartache, disappointment, failure, mistake, and past hurt to be the stepping stones to your purpose. I believe that every life experience, whether good or bad, are lessons to prepare us for our purpose. We've all heard the phrase "what didn't kill you made you stronger." This is absolutely true, depending on how you view your pain. If you see yourself as victorious and not a victim, then reclaim the power over your life. It's important to ensure that you don't stay in a state of being victimized. What happened to you was wrong and painful, but you are not your circumstances nor the bad things that have happened to you. You and I are warriors, and warriors never quit! They strategize how to win the next battle. In the Bible, 2 Chronicles 20:15 reads that this battle is not yours, but God's.

For me, understanding my worth and measuring my pain correctly took years. Truthfully, writing books have been a form of healing and hope for me. In them, I shared my pain, hurt, and heartaches with the world to inspire others. I had no idea they would bring healing to my soul; therefore, you never know how your story could impact others in a positive way. Through this journal, I invite you to explore your purpose through your pain. I invite you to track the process God is making in your life so that one day you can look back and marvel at how far you've come. My only hope is that you don't quit. Your existence is worth fighting for.

DAILY REFLECTION 1
BELIEVE AGAIN

"Rest in the Lord, and wait patiently for him: fret not thyself because of him who prospereth in his way, because of the man who bringeth wicked devices to pass." (Psalm 37:7)

Have the courage to believe in your faith again. The enemy wants you to abort your faith, because that's your lifeline and source of strength. If he can keep you from believing again, he will keep you in bondage and distracted from your God-given purpose. Remember, God created each of us with a divine purpose. You were created to make an impact in the earth with your gifts, talents, and treasures. You're not an accident, no matter how you were conceived or from whom you came. God makes no mistakes. Be determined to take every heartache, setback, rejection, and pain and use them for your purpose. Claim freedom over your mind, family, and finances. Your freedom begins today!

TOO HURT TO CRY

Aileen Cunningham

DAILY REFLECTION 2
TRUST THE PROCESS

"Now faith is confidence in what we hope for and assurance about what we do not see." (Hebrews 11:1)

Remove "I feel" from your vocabulary. It can be misleading to your faith. Oftentimes, how we feel isn't a true description of our current state of being. The words "I feel" can cause you to misunderstand the timing of God. If not checked soon enough, it will destroy your faith and belief that God has His best interests in store for you. That's why in the Bible, the Lord told the prophet Jeremiah, "For I know the plans I have for you, declares the Lord, plans for good and not evil, to give you a future and a hope." (Jeremiah 29:11) That means God has good things planned for us.

Replace "I feel" with "I'm trusting." By doing so, you're training your spirit to react by faith and not by what you see or your emotions. "I'm trusting" simply means that the situation is completely out of your control and the outcome is totally up to God. For example, I'm trusting that my heavenly Father hears me when I pray, and that all things are working together for my good.

"And we know that in all things God works for the good of those who love him, who have been called according to his purpose." (Romans 8:28)

Let's practice this together. List three things you are trusting God for today.

I'm trusting God for ...

1. _____

2. _____

3. _____

TOO HURT TO CRY

Aileen Cunningham

DAILY REFLECTION 3
FOCUS ON YOUR TALENTS

"Keep this book of the law always on your lips: meditate on it day and night, so that you may be careful to do everything written in it. Then you will be prosperous and successful." (Joshua 1:8)

Today, focus on your talents. Each of us are given a talent or several talents which make us unique. Focusing on your talent(s) should bring you joy. For example, I'm talented at baking cupcakes, entrepreneurship, and cooking. I find that when I spend time cooking, I have a sense of relief. I believe we should develop and use our gifts and talents to prosper in life. Don't focus on other people's gifts; rather, focus on what comes easy to you. Be careful not to compare your gifts and talents to others. What God has given you is enough. What you have in your hands is enough because God made us unique.

Remember, prosperity and success aren't about material things or how much money you have. They're about using all your gifts and talents to make an impact in the earth. They're about dying empty after you've completed the work that God intended for you. That's why knowing your purpose and who you are extremely important. Knowing who you are will help you decide how to your use and handle your gifts wisely.

List three things you enjoy doing that come easy to you.

1. _____

2. _____

3. _____

In the space below, write how you can spend time perfecting those talents. How and why do they bring you joy?

_____

_____

_____

_____

TOO HURT TO CRY

Aileen Cunningham

DAILY REFLECTION 4
FIGHT THROUGH THE STORM WITH THE RIGHT TOOLS

Have you ever woken up feeling like you have been hit by a car emotionally? You may have had eight hours of sleep, but you still felt drained. It could be that you're emotionally drained or entering a storm with the wrong tools for fighting.

2 Corinthians 10:4 reads,

"For the weapons of our warfare are not carnal, but mighty through God to the pulling down of strong holds."

Today, examine what weapons you are using in this storm. Is it overeating, shopping, drinking alcohol, sex, or seeking fulfillment in a relationship? Whatever it is that takes you away from the presence of God, start praying that He gives you the strength to remove it from your life. Don't invest your faith in things or people; however, invest it in the power of prayer and meditation because your strength comes from them.

List three people from the Bible you admire and why. Spend today mediating on them.

1. _____

2. _____

3. _____

TOO HURT TO CRY

Aileen Cunningham

DAILY REFLECTION 5
SEE BEYOND THAT MOUNTAIN

Don't allow that mountain to consume your mind, time, or energy. Daily, we all have a different type of mountain to face. The key to making it through each day with joy is by not allowing that which you don't have control over to drain you.

Today, list five things that you have the power to change in your circumstances. For example, if you want to lose weight, you have the power to start that change by eating healthier. Take baby steps toward this goal.

1. _____

2. _____

3. _____

4. _____

5. _____

DAILY REFLECTION 6

GIVE THANKS

"Be thankful in all circumstances, for this is God's will for you who belong to Christ Jesus." (1 Thessalonians 5:18)

I found that on days when I feel at my worst to try to focus on the good things in my life. Oftentimes, my daughter was the number-one thing for which I would give thanks. Think of one thing for which you could thank God today. Write it down. When you feel discouraged, read it as a reminder that you have one thing for which to be thankful.

List three things that are good in your life, then spend the day mediating and thanking God for them.

1. _____

2. _____

3. _____

TOO HURT TO CRY

Aileen Cunningham

DAILY REFLECTION 7
PUSH PASS THE CHAOS

"Some of the crowed advised Alexander to speak, since the Jews had pushed him forward; and Alexander motioned with his hand and intended to make a defense to the people."

(Acts 19:33)

Oftentimes, our lives are consumed with constant distractions. We're distracted by our phones, work, relationships, and much more. Today, try to remove the chaos or noise throughout your day.

List three things that you could remove or limit that would bring peace and calm to your day. Remove or limit them, and at the end of the day, reflect on how your day was different.

1. _____

2. _____

3. _____

DAILY REFLECTION 8
TAKE CARE OF YOU

"Confirming the souls of the disciples, and exhorting them to continue in the faith, and that we must through much tribulation enter into the kingdom of God." (Acts 14:22)

Self-care is one of the things that we often overlook. As a single mother, I find myself taking care of others and not myself. Now, I realize how important it is to practice self-care. If you don't take care of yourself, helping others becomes impossible. I remind myself of the phrase "you can't pour from an empty cup", which means you must make yourself a priority so that you can be effective in the lives of those you care so much about.

Today, list three ways in which you would like to make yourself a priority. Whether it's getting your nails done, planning a spa day, exercising, or taking yourself to dinner, take care of you today!

1. _____

TOO HURT TO CRY

2. _____

3. _____

Aileen Cunningham

TOO HURT TO CRY

DAILY REFLECTION 9
FREE YOUR SPIRIT

"Therefore, since we have these promises, dear friends, let us purify ourselves from everything that contaminates body and spirit, perfecting holiness out of reverence for God." (2 Corinthians 7:1)

What does freeing your spirit mean? It means removing everything that causes you spiritual constipation – what blocks you from hearing from God. Basically, it's a spiritual detox to cleanse yourself from within.

Identity the areas in your spiritual life that you could detoxify to make yourself spiritually healthy. List them and spend the day praying 2 Corinthians 7:1, which reads,

"Having therefore these promises, dearly beloved, let us cleanse ourselves from all filthiness of the flesh and spirit, perfecting holiness in the fear of God.

Ask God for the wisdom to overcome in these areas and the discipline to do so.

1. _____

2. _____

3. _____

4. _____

Aileen Cunningham

TOO HURT TO CRY

DAILY REFLECTION 10
REBUILD YOUR FAITH

"For I know the plans I have for you, says the Lord. They are plans for good and not for disaster, to give you a future and a hope?" (Jeremiah 29:11)

Today's reflection of rebuilding your faith is one of my most challenging requests, for it is a daily process. Oftentimes, faith is rebuilt through life's challenges, storms, and hardships. If you're currently in a storm, take this opportunity to lean on your faith and trust God through this process. I'm a witness that every hardship I've encountered was a test to strengthen my faith.

What is faith? It is having complete trust or confidence in something that you can't see. It also means trusting or having hope in God through the unknown process.

Knowing that God has good plans for you helps build your faith and trust in Him. It's one of our greatest weapons as believers. The Bible reads in Hebrews 11:6 that "but without faith it's impossible to please God".

Don't be discouraged if you've found yourself in a strange place spiritually, not knowing which direction to turn or go. This is the perfect opportunity for you to give your heart and concerns to God. Allow Him to carry you through this test; therefore, when you come out, you can tell others what rebuilding your faith and trusting in Him means.

List three areas in which you need total faith in God. Openly speak each area aloud, then ask God to help you trust that everything is working together for your good (Romans 8:28). Keep covering those areas in prayer until you see change. Remember, rebuilding your faith is not an overnight process. It's a daily process to strengthen you for your life's journey.

1. _____

2. _____

3. _____

Aileen Cunningham

TOO HURT TO CRY

DAILY REFLECTION 11
TRY AGAIN

What vision has God given you that you've put on the back burner because it failed every time you tried to bring it to life?

Habakkuk 2:2 reads,

"...Write the the vision and make it plain tablets, that he may run that reads it."

This vision is for a future time. It describes the end, and it will be fulfilled. If it seems slow in coming to fruition, wait patiently, for it will surely happen. It will not be delayed.

Today, write the vision or visions that God has assigned you to complete to make an impact in the world. They are part of your God-given assignment. Write them down and set a realistic goal and date for completing them . We must plan to be successful and obey the assignment from our Heavenly Father. Trust God that He will make provision for the vision.

God will supply all that you need for your vision to come to pass. It's not our responsibility to figure out the how, but *why* God placed the vision in your heart. Once you understand the why, then you will be encouraged to push forward with knowing *how* the vision is going to come to pass. Apply your faith to trust God during this process, and in due time the vision will come fourth and accomplish everything that God intended for it.

Aileen Cunningham

DAILY REFLECTION 12
REMOVE ANY DOUBT

"For God hath not given us the spirit of fear; but of power, and of love, and of a sound mind." (2 Timothy 1:7)

It's hard to believe God's plan for your life when doubt is present. I believe the Bible warns us about doubt because it drives out faith. We know that it's impossible to please God or have hope in God without faith. The worldly standard wants us to believe in our own strength and remove God from the equation. Today, list three areas in your life from which you could remove doubt. After identifying them, spend time praying that God will strengthen your faith in those areas.

1. _____

2. _____

3. _____

Aileen Cunningham

TOO HURT TO CRY

DAILY REFLECTION 13
PREPARE YOUR MIND FOR YOUR HARVEST

"All the commandments which I command thee this day shall ye observe to do, that ye may live, and multiply, and go in and possess the land which the Lord sware unto your fathers." (Deuteronomy 8:1-20)

I know you've encountered some challenges in your life's journey. It hasn't been easy to stand in the mist of them. At times, you couldn't stand; you had to kneel and allow your heavenly Father to carry you. It was during those difficult times that He was preparing you for this moment: the moment of your harvest. It was God who gave you the wealth and sustained you.

In 2013, I started reading Deuteronomy chapter 8, where Moses tells the children of Israel about entering into their harvest season and warns them of what would happen if they forget to keep His commandments. I couldn't understand why God lead me there. This chapter reminds us that God allowed us to go through every test and trial so that He might humble us, and know what was in our hearts and whether we would keep His commandments. In other words, He was drawing our hearts back to Him. He was revealing that He is God and has complete control over our situations. As your seasons change be encouraged to enjoy your harvest, but always remember that God brought you through!

Deuteronomy 8:18 reads,

"And you shall remember the Lord your God, for it is He who gives you power to get wealth, that He may establish His covenant which He swore to your fathers, as it is this day."

Today, find three books that you can read to encourage your heart as you prepare for your harvest season. When you feel discouraged, read one of them to encourage your heart and spirit. The following are some of my favorite books for encouragement:

- *Destiny,* by T.D. Jakes
- *In Pursuit of Purpose,* by Dr. Myles Munroe
- *Life Without Limits,* by Nick Vujicic
- *The Psychology of Winning: "We Always Win",* by Calvin Scott

Aileen Cunningham

TOO HURT TO CRY

DAILY REFLECTION 14
FORGIVE THOSE WHO'VE HURT YOU

"For if you forgive other people when they sin against you, your heavenly Father will also forgive you." (Matthew 6:14)

As believers, the power of forgiveness is one of the most powerful weapons that we can use. Forgiveness isn't about being weak or forgetting the pain someone caused you. It's about freeing your heart and spirit. Making the decision to forgive isn't about the other person. It's simply for your healing. Failure to forgive breeds bitterness, sickness, and a hardened heart. God never intended for us to have a hardened heart.

Think of forgiveness as a medicine used to heal the wounds of our past hurts. This would allow the blood around your heart to flow freely so that you can help free others of their pain. Draw a picture of a heart. Ask God to give you the courage to forgive all those who have hurt you. Write verses of Scripture about forgiveness around the heart, then put your name in the middle of the heart and declare your healing.

TOO HURT TO CRY

Aileen Cunningham

DAILY REFLECTION 15
IT'S ALL WORKING TOGETHER FOR YOUR GOOD

"And we know that God causes everything to work together for the good of those who love God and are called according to his purpose for them." Romans 8:28

I know you may not see it right now, but I'm a living witness that ALL things will work together for your good. Even when you're in the storms of life, they're working together for your good. During difficult times, it's important that you build yourself up with positive thoughts and remember what our God has promised us.

When you're being stretched or tested, it isn't easy to encourage yourself because you're in pain. Please don't allow that pain to draw your heart and mind away from God. From my own personal experiences, I urge you not to search for worldly things like alcohol, sex, or bad relationships as temporary fixes for the pain. It will only leave you more broken and hurt. Avoid seeking after what the world offers you. Rather, take your brokenness and hurt to God and allow Him to strengthen you. Allow Him to carry you and cover your pain.

Worldly things only cause you more pain in the end. It's like you not going to see a doctor when you're physically hurt. You have all the symptoms that you've been injured, but you ignore them. Over time, they become worse; therefore, it's best that you to talk to the Great Physician, our heavenly Father, who is the ultimate healer.

Today, I encourage you to create your future of faith and hope. Work on creating a vision board for your life. I started by taking photos of what I desired for my life. Then I printed them and placed them on a blank whiteboard, which I hung in my bedroom so I could see myself coming out victorious every day when I wake up. You must see yourself coming out of each storm, have faith that everything is working together for your good, and openly giving thanks to God for already working things out (1 Thessalonians 5:18). When you feel discouraged, look at your vision board for encouragement.

"For everything there is a season, a time for every activity under heaven." (Ecclesiastes 3:1)

TOO HURT TO CRY

Aileen Cunningham

DAILY REFLECTION 16
CHOOSE TO TRUST

"Trust in the Lord with all your heart; do not depend on your own understanding. Seek his will in all you do, and he will show you which path to take." (Proverbs 3:5-6)

Today, choose to trust God with your life. At the time of this publication I'm preparing to have surgery, and I must trust God that He is leading my path. I understand that the processes of life can cause you to lose focus on what really matters, which is fulfilling your assignment and purpose. The only way for you to do this is by seeking the Creator of life, our heavenly Father. Ask Him for direction and choose to trust in His plan for your life.

Note: For tomorrow's reflection, you will need a box of cake mix and the ingredients to bake a cake. **Stop – please don't read ahead! Patiently wait until tomorrow.**

List three things for which you need to trust God. Be detailed in your writing today. Ensure that you are clear about why you need to trust God in these areas. Then, find your favorite verse of Scripture and place these items in your bible. If you don't have a bible, this is the perfect time to ask for one. When your heart is heavy, read the items aloud to encourage your heart. Make today great, because it's a gift from God.

TOO HURT TO CRY

Aileen Cunningham

DAILY REFLECTION 17
DON'T ACCEPT THE VALLEY

"For the Lord your God is bringing you into a good land, a land of brooks of water, of fountains and springs, that flow out of valleys and hills; ⁸a land of wheat and barley, of vines and fig trees and pomegranates, a land of olive oil and honey; ⁹a land in which you will eat bread without scarcity, in which you will lack nothing; a land whose stones are iron and out of whose hills you will dig copper." (Deuteronomy 8:7-9)

Bake something sweet. Start by reading the instructions on the back on the cake mix box. Ensure that you have all the ingredients on the table. After you review the instructions, start baking your cake. **Stop – don't read any further until your cake is baked.**

How did your cake turn out? I hope it turned out well. Why did I have you bake a cake today? I wanted you to trust the process of baking. Oftentimes in life, we forget to trust the process through which God is allowing us to go. We stop believing and trusting when the process is painful. Today, I encourage you to see yourself as the ingredients that God is using to bake something great! Where you are in life right now is not the finished product. Allow God to finish what He started in you.

As painful as it might be, don't rush the process. Pray that God gives you the strength and peace to endure it. See yourself as the cake rising to become something great. Each ingredient you used to bake your cake played a major role in developing something sweet. If one ingredient was removed or forgotten, it would have changed the outcome of your cake.

Now that you understand the baking process, see God as the baker. He is in complete control of ensuring that the ingredients get into the bowl, the baking pan, and the oven; setting the oven's temperature; and checking for when to remove the cake. His timing is perfect; if He removes you too soon, then you won't be properly baked. Do you know what happens when a cake is not properly baked all the way through? It's not solid enough to eat. God is preparing you to be solid enough to stand against every trial and test you will encounter. Stay in the fire long enough until He removes you. Remember, you are not alone in the fire. He's right there with you, preparing you for something great!

"Be strong and courageous. Do not be afraid or terrified because of them. For the Lord your God goes with you; he will never leave you nor forsake you." (Deuteronomy 31:6)

Aileen Cunningham

TOO HURT TO CRY

DAILY REFLECTION 18
RISE TO THE TOP

Warrior, it's time for you to rise up! 2 Chronicles 20:5 reads,

"For this battle is not yours but God's."

One of the hardest lessons I had to learn during my struggles was that I was wasting energy trying to fight my battles in my own strength. God never intended for us to fight our battles alone. Deuteronomy 31:6 reads,

"He will neither fail you nor abandon you."

Today, identify three ways in which you could reclaim your strength. For example, I started reclaiming my strength by healing my body through eating right, working out, and focusing on my purpose. Trust God that He is fighting every battle on your behalf. You are not alone, for He has his angels all around you fighting on your behalf.

TOO HURT TO CRY

1. _____

2. _____

3. _____

Aileen Cunningham

TOO HURT TO CRY

DAILY REFLECTION 19
BELIEVE

"But let him ask in faith. With no doubting, for the one who doubts is like a wave of the sea that is driven and tossed by the wind." (James 1:6)

This is your opportunity to build your faith and believe in God. What are you believing God for? Do you have any doubts about what you're expecting from Him?

Today, list three things you're expecting God to do in your life. No matter how big or small your desires are, believe that God is able to bring them to pass.

In the Bible, Ephesians reads,

"Now to Him who is able to do exceedingly abundantly above all that we ask or think, according to the power that works in us."

TOO HURT TO CRY

1. _____

2. _____

3. _____

Aileen Cunningham

TOO HURT TO CRY

DAILY REFLECTION 20
TAKE CHARGE

"Casting all your care upon him; for He cares for you." (1 Peter 5:7)

Today, list five things that are heavy on your heart. Cover them in prayer and ask God to give you the grace you need to push forward. It's already done, and it is so. Amen.

1. _____

2. _____

3. _____

4. _____

5. _____

TOO HURT TO CRY

Aileen Cunningham

DAILY REFLECTION 21
MOVE FORWARD BY FAITH

It's time for you to move forward from your past hurts. Moving forward isn't ignoring the people or things that caused you to be hurt. Moving forward is acknowledging that your journey is preparing you for your life's work. Today, I encourage you to see the pain of your process as preparation for your purpose. You are stronger, wiser, and more powerful because of what you encountered.

One day, you will look back and rejoice for how far you've come. During that time of reflection, remember to give God thanks for His faithfulness. Psalms 118:1 reads,

"Give thanks to the Lord, for he is good; his love endures forever."

Never allow what the enemy intended to break you to keep you from giving God praise. He's kept you when you didn't want to be kept.

Today, write your three-step plan for moving forward. What have you learned from your 21-day journey that can help you push forward?

1. _____

2. _____

3. _____

TOO HURT TO CRY

Aileen Cunningham

SUMMARY

SAY IT LOUD. SPEAK LIFE OVER YOUR MIND AND BODY

Words have power. Solomon declares in Proverbs 18:21 that "Death and life are in the power of the tongue; and those who love it will eat its fruit." You now have the wisdom to allow God to heal you from the inside out, starting with the words you speak over yourself.

Thank you for allowing me to share my heart and experiences with you. I'm hopeful that every dark day I faced prepared me to write this journal to encourage, guide, and impact your life in a positive way. Now I know that I survived the storms for you, and I'm glad I did! Your life has meaning, so please don't quit getting back up again. This, too, shall pass. *2 Corinthians 4:17-18* reads,

"for our present troubles are small and won't last very long. Yet they produce for us a glory that vastly outweighs them and will last forever. So, we don't look at the troubles we can

see now; ¹⁸rather, we fix our gaze on things that cannot be seen. For the things, we see now will soon be gone, but the things we can't see will last forever."

Tomorrow is a new day. Be encouraged to stay in the race.

TOO HURT TO CRY

Aileen Cunningham

www.ingramcontent.com/pod-product-compliance
Lightning Source LLC
Chambersburg PA
CBHW070133100426
42744CB00009B/1824